Country Christmas

COOKBOOK

ideals

Ideals Publishing Corp.
Milwaukee, Wisconsin

Contents

Appetizers 4

Beverages 9

Soups 12

Salads 17

Main Dishes 22

Casseroles 31

Side Dishes 38

Brunch 44

Breads 49

Desserts 54

Kitchen Gifts 60

Index 64

Our sincere thanks to the following for their cooperation and help in supplying selected recipes from their test kitchens and files: American Dairy Association; American Seafood Institute; American Spice Trade Association; Borden Inc.; California Olive Industry; National Fisheries Institute; National Pork Producer's Council; North Carolina Yam Commission; Ocean Spray; Potato Board; Sea Grant College Program/Texas Agricultural Extension Service; Stokely-Van Camp, Inc.; Washington State Apple Commission.

Director of Publishing Patricia Pingry
Managing Editor Marybeth Owens
Cookbook Editor Naomi Galbreath
Art Director William Scholz
Photographer Gerald Koser
Editorial Assistants Marjorie Friess, Linda Robinson
Typography Kim Kaczanowski

ISBN 0-8249-3032-0
Copyright © MCMLXXXIV by Ideals Publishing Corp.
All rights reserved.
Printed and bound in the United States of America.

Published by Ideals Publishing Corporation
11315 Watertown Plank Road
Milwaukee, Wisconsin 53226
Published simultaneously in Canada

Cover Recipes
Baked Ham with Cherry Glaze, 27
Christmas Stollen, 49
Pumpkin Cheese Pie, 59
Little Christmas Cookies, 63

Christmas Stollen, 49

APPETIZERS

Chicken Drumettes

Makes 36 servings

36 chicken wings
5 ounces soy sauce
1 teaspoon Dijon-style mustard
4 tablespoons brown sugar
½ teaspoon garlic powder

Cut chicken wings in pieces. Set aside bony tips for soup or other use. In a shallow pan, mix soy sauce, brown sugar, mustard, and garlic powder until well blended. Put in the wings and turn to coat. Marinate for 2 hours in the refrigerator. Bake in the same pan for 1 hour at 375 ° F. Baste frequently with pan juices. Serve hot.

Sharp Gouda Spread

Makes about 1½ cups

1 baby Gouda cheese (8 ounces)
½ cup finely chopped smoked sliced beef
¼ cup sour cream
2 tablespoons pickle relish
2 teaspoons horseradish

With a round cookie cutter, cut a round of wax from the top of the cheese. Carefully scoop cheese from shell, keeping shell intact. In a small mixing bowl, beat cheese until smooth. Add beef, sour cream, pickle relish, and horseradish; blend well. Pack cheese mixture into Gouda shell.

Pineapple Cheese Ball

Makes 1 cheese ball

2 packages (8 ounces *each*) cream cheese, softened
1 can (3½ ounces) crushed pineapple, drained
2 cups chopped pecans, divided
¼ cup finely chopped green pepper
2 tablespoons finely chopped onion
1 tablespoon seasoned salt
Pineapple, cherries, or parsley for garnish

In a medium bowl, beat cream cheese until smooth. Stir in crushed pineapple, 1 cup pecans, green pepper, onion, and salt. Shape cheese mixture into a ball. Roll in remaining nuts. Wrap in plastic wrap or foil. Refrigerate at least 6 hours. Garnish with fruit or parsley.

Creamy Seafood Spread

Makes 2 cups

1 package (8 ounces) cream
   cheese
¼ cup finely chopped onion
¼ cup finely chopped celery
½ cup sour cream
1 can (4¼ ounces) broken
   shrimp
1 can (6½ ounces) crab meat
½ cup cocktail sauce

In a small bowl, combine cream cheese, onion, celery, and sour cream; mix well. Spread neatly on a small serving plate. In the same bowl, mix together crab and shrimp; spread over cream cheese mixture. Spread cocktail sauce over top.

Ripe Olive Spread

Makes 1⅓ cups

1 cup firmly packed chopped
   ripe olives
⅓ cup finely chopped walnuts
3 tablespoons mayonnaise

In a small bowl, mix together ripe olives, walnuts, and mayonnaise. Use as a spread for sandwiches, hors d'oeuvres, or as a dip.

Puffy Cheese Appetizers

Makes 35 servings

1 package (10 ounces) frozen
   pastry shells
1 egg, lightly beaten
1 tablespoon sesame seed
1 tablespoon butter
½ cup finely chopped onion
¼ cup finely chopped fresh
   parsley
½ teaspoon salt
2 cups lightly packed shredded
   Monterey Jack cheese

Thaw pastry shells. Preheat oven to 450° F. On a lightly floured surface, arrange 2 rows of 3 shells each, overlapping shells slightly. Roll and pat into a 10 x 14-inch rectangle. Transfer to a 10 x 15-inch rimmed baking sheet. Prick bottom of pastry with a fork. Brush with egg; sprinkle with sesame seed. Bake uncovered for 15 minutes. In a small pan, melt butter. Add onion; sauté until limp but not brown. Add parsley; sauté 1 minute. Remove from heat. Stir in cheese. Spoon parsley mixture over baked pastry to within ½ inch of the edge. Return to oven; bake uncovered until cheese is melted and pastry is brown, about 5 minutes. Cut into 2-inch squares.

Fruit and Nut Nibble

Makes about 5½ cups

½ pound raw cashews
½ pound pecans
½ pound almonds
1 cup chopped dried apples
1 cup flaked coconut
1 cup raisins
1 cup dried apricots, chopped
1 cup carob chips, optional

Mix together all ingredients. Store covered.

This nibble is a nutritious, quick-energy snack that is equally appropriate for the lunchbox or the banquet table.

Crab Stuffed Mushrooms

Makes 36 stuffed mushrooms

3 dozen large whole fresh mushrooms
1 can (6½ ounces) crab meat, drained and flaked
½ cup mayonnaise
1 tablespoon chopped fresh parsley
1 tablespoon pimiento, chopped
1 teaspoon chopped olives
¼ teaspoon dry mustard

Preheat oven to 375° F. Wash and dry mushrooms. Remove stems; reserve for another use. Mix remaining ingredients. Fill each cap with crabmeat mixture. Place stuffed mushrooms on a cookie sheet. Bake 8 to 10 minutes.

Stuffed Tiny Tomatoes

Makes about 70 stuffed tomatoes

½ pound potatoes
¾ cup chopped ripe olives, divided
½ cup chopped cucumber
1 hard-cooked egg, chopped
1 green onion, finely chopped
2 tablespoons mayonnaise
2 tablespoons sour cream
2 teaspoons Dijon-style mustard
1 teaspoon cider vinegar
1 teaspoon minced fresh dillweed, or ¼ teaspoon dried
Salt and pepper to taste
About 70 to 75 cherry tomatoes

In a large saucepan, cook potatoes in boiling salted water until tender, about 30 to 35 minutes. Drain; cool, peel, and dice. In a mixing bowl, stir together potatoes, ½ cup chopped olives, cucumber, egg, onion, mayonnaise, sour cream, mustard, vinegar, and dill. Season to taste with salt and pepper; set aside. Cut a thin slice from stem end of each tomato. Scoop pulp and seeds from center with a small spoon or melon baller, or cut a deep "X" from top of tomato almost to bottom. Carefully pull tomato open and scoop out pulp and seeds. Fill tomatoes with potato salad mixture. Garnish tops with remaining chopped olives.

Fruit and Nut Nibble
Crisp Vegetable Medley, 17

Appetizers

Simple Salmon Pâté

Makes 3 pounds

1 pound salmon, cooked fresh
  or canned
2 packages (8 ounces *each*)
  cream cheese, softened
2 tablespoons chili sauce
2 tablespoons chopped fresh
  parsley
1 small onion, minced
½ teaspoon hot sauce
  Dash garlic powder
  Parsley for garnish

In a mixing bowl, blend all ingredients until smooth. Pack into a small oiled bowl. Chill overnight. Unmold and garnish with parsley.

Sherried Chicken Livers and Mushrooms

Makes 4 servings

1 chicken bouillon cube
1 cup boiling water
2 tablespoons butter *or*
  margarine
½ pound fresh mushrooms,
  sliced
3 tablespoons minced onion
½ pound chicken livers, halved
1 tablespoon flour
½ teaspoon salt
¼ teaspoon thyme
2 tablespoons dry sherry
2 tablespoons chopped fresh
  parsley

Dissolve bouillon cube in boiling water. In a large skillet, melt butter. Add mushrooms and onion; sauté until golden, about 5 minutes. Add chicken livers and sauté until browned, about 10 minutes. Stir in flour, salt, and thyme. Gradually blend bouillon into liver mixture. Add sherry; stir and cook until thickened. Sprinkle with parsley. Serve over toast points.

Snappy Cheese Wedges

Makes 48 wedges

12 slices white bread
½ cup process Cheddar cheese
  spread
¼ teaspoon Tabasco
¼ teaspoon prepared mustard
  Rolled anchovies, optional

Preheat oven to 400° F. Remove crusts from bread. Slice on the diagonals to form 4 wedges from each slice. In a small bowl, mix cheese spread, Tabasco, and mustard until well blended. Spread on bread wedges. Bake for 5 minutes or until cheese is bubbly. Top with rolled anchovies. Serve hot.

BEVERAGES

Hot Mulled Cider _____

Makes 10 servings

½ cup brown sugar
¼ teaspoon salt
2 quarts cider
1 teaspoon whole allspice
1 teaspoon whole cloves
1 cinnamon stick, about 3
   inches long
Dash nutmeg

In a saucepan, combine brown sugar, salt, and cider; mix well. Tie whole spices in a small piece of cheesecloth; add to cider with nutmeg. Over medium heat, bring cider mixture to a boil. Reduce heat. Cover; simmer 20 minutes. Remove spices.

Cranberry Scoop _____

Makes 6 to 8 servings

2 cups cranberry juice cocktail
16 fresh *or* frozen whole
   strawberries
1 banana, sliced
8 ounces frozen vanilla yogurt

In a blender, combine juice, strawberries, banana, and frozen yogurt. Blend until mixture is smooth.

Grapefruit Strawberry Frappé _____

Makes 4 to 6 servings

¾ cup unsweetened pineapple
   juice, chilled
10 fresh or frozen whole
   strawberries
2 tablespoons sugar
8 ounces vanilla yogurt
3 cups pink grapefruit juice,
   chilled

In a blender, place pineapple juice, strawberries, and sugar. Process until smooth. Add yogurt and grapefruit juice. Process until blended.

Cappuccino _____

Whipped cream
Ground cinnamon *or* nutmeg
Freshly brewed coffee
Sugar to taste

In a coffee cup, place a dollop of whipped cream. Add a dash of cinnamon or nutmeg. Pour coffee into the cup. Add sugar and additional spice as desired.

Christmas Punch

Makes 12 servings

¾ cup sugar
½ teaspoon cinnamon
¼ teaspoon nutmeg
¼ teaspoon salt
2 cups boiling water
2 bottles (16 ounces *each*)
   cranberry juice cocktail
2 cans (6 ounces) frozen
   pineapple juice concentrate
1 cup cold water
2 bottles (12 ounces *each*)
   carbonated water
   Ice cubes, optional

In a mixing bowl, stir together sugar, cinnamon, nutmeg, and salt. Pour in boiling water; stir until sugar is dissolved. Chill thoroughly. To serve, pour into punch bowl. Add remaining ingredients; stir to mix. Add ice if desired.

Coffee Nog

Makes 10 servings

2 quarts eggnog, chilled
¼ cup firmly packed brown
   sugar
2 tablespoons instant coffee
   powder
¼ teaspoon cinnamon
½ cup coffee liqueur, optional
½ cup bourbon *or* brandy,
   optional
1 cup whipping cream
¼ cup confectioners' sugar
1 teaspoon vanilla
   Nutmeg
   Cinnamon sticks

In a large bowl, combine eggnog, brown sugar, instant coffee, and cinnamon. Beat until sugar and coffee are dissolved. Stir in liqueur and bourbon, if desired. Chill. In a small bowl, combine cream, confectioners' sugar, and vanilla. Beat until stiff. Pour eggnog mixture into a punch bowl. Top with whipped cream. Sprinkle with nutmeg; serve with cinnamon sticks.

Orange Pineapple Shake

Makes 6 to 8 servings

2 cups orange juice, chilled
1 can (8 ounces) crushed
   pineapple, packed in its
   own juice
1½ cups vanilla ice cream

In a blender, combine orange juice, pineapple, and ice cream. Blend until smooth and frothy.

SOUPS

New England Clam Chowder

Makes 6 servings

1 tablespoon butter
¾ cup chopped onion
2 cups peeled, cubed potatoes
1 teaspoon salt
¼ teaspoon pepper
1 teaspoon crumbled crisp
　bacon
1 cup water
2 cans (6½ ounces *each*) minced
　clams, undrained
1 cup evaporated skim milk

In a large saucepan, melt butter. Add onion; sauté until softened. Stir in potatoes, salt, pepper, bacon, and 1 cup water. Cover; simmer 30 minutes or until potatoes are tender. Stir in clams in their juice, and milk. Heat and stir until bubbly.

Beef and Barley Soup

Makes 12 servings

2 tablespoons vegetable oil
1 pound boneless beef, cut in
　½-inch cubes
½ cup minced onion
½ cup pearl barley
1 pound beef bones
1 carrot, cut in ½-inch slices
1 stalk celery, cut in ½-inch
　slices
½ cup cubed turnip, rutabaga *or*
　parsnip
2 tablespoons chopped fresh
　parsley
1 bay leaf
1 tablespoon salt
3 quarts water

In a large pot, heat oil; sauté beef and onion until beef is browned. Add barley. Sauté for 5 minutes, stirring constantly. Add remaining ingredients. Cover and simmer for 2 hours. Discard bones before serving. Can be prepared ahead and frozen.

Cheesy Cream of Potato Soup

Makes 4 servings

4 peeled medium potatoes
2 bacon slices, diced
¼ cup minced onion
2 tablespoons butter *or* margarine
1 tablespoon chopped fresh parsley
2 teaspoons salt
½ teaspoon nutmeg
　Dash cayenne pepper
¼ teaspoon dry mustard
1 teaspoon Worcestershire sauce
3 cups milk
½ cup lightly packed shredded Swiss *or* American cheese

In a large saucepan, simmer potatoes in water to cover until tender, about 30 minutes; drain. In a skillet, sauté bacon and onion over low heat until bacon is brown and onion is tender; drain fat. In a mixing bowl, mash potatoes. Add bacon, onion, butter, parsley, salt, nutmeg, cayenne, mustard, and Worcestershire sauce; blend well. Blend in milk. Stirring constantly over low heat, bring to serving temperature. Sprinkle with cheese. Serve immediately.

Oyster Bisque

Makes 4 servings

1 dozen shucked large raw oysters, diced
1 cup oyster liquor
3 cups milk
1 cup heavy cream
1 slice onion
2 stalks celery
1 sprig parsley
1 bay leaf
⅓ cup butter *or* margarine, melted
⅓ cup flour
1¾ teaspoons salt
½ teaspoon hot pepper sauce
　Chopped chives

In a medium saucepan, place oysters and oyster liquor. Slowly bring to a boil. Transfer oysters and liquor to a separate bowl. In the same saucepan, place milk, cream, onion, celery, parsley, and bay leaf. Gently heat milk mixture just until tiny bubbles begin to appear at edge of pan. Remove milk from heat; strain. In a large saucepan, blend butter with flour, salt, and hot pepper sauce. Slowly stir in scalded milk. Stir over low heat until thick. Add oysters and oyster liquor. Heat to serving temperature. Garnish with chopped chives.

Note: Turn leftover vegetables into delicious, easily-made cream soups. Heat 1 cup pureed cooked vegetables, 2 cups milk, 1 tablespoon butter, and seasonings to taste.

Mild Onion Soup

Makes 8 servings

6 tablespoons butter
6 cups thinly sliced onions
6 cans (14 ounces *each*)
  beef broth
1 teaspoon salt
½ cup lightly packed, shredded
  Swiss cheese
1 cup plain croutons
  Grated Parmesan cheese

In a large pot, melt butter. Sauté onion until golden. Add bouillon and salt. Simmer 1 hour. To serve, place 1 teaspoon Swiss cheese in bottom of each soup bowl or mug; then ladle in hot soup. Top with croutons and a sprinkling of Parmesan cheese.

Lentil Soup

Makes 8 to 10 servings

1 pound lentils
1 onion, chopped
2 stalks celery, chopped
3 cloves garlic, minced
½ cup olive oil
2 tablespoons tomato paste
2 whole cloves
½ bay leaf
  Salt and pepper to taste

Rinse lentils in colander under cold running water. Soak for 1 hour in lukewarm water. Drain; transfer to a large saucepan. Add 2 quarts water, onion, celery, garlic, olive oil, tomato paste, cloves, bay leaf, salt, and pepper. Bring to a boil over moderate heat. Reduce heat, cover, and simmer for 30 minutes. Check the soup occasionally, adding more water if necessary. Soup should be fairly thick. Pour into a heated tureen and serve.

Cheddar Cheese Soup

Makes 8 servings

¼ cup butter *or* margarine
½ cup flour
6 cups chicken stock
½ cup finely chopped onion
½ cup finely chopped carrot
½ pound Cheddar cheese, cubed
1½ cups milk
12 ounces beer
½ cup chopped fresh parsley
½ teaspoon salt
  Dash white pepper

In a large saucepan, melt butter. Blend in flour. Cook, stirring, until flour is brown. Slowly add stock, stirring and blending with a wire whisk. Simmer until slightly thickened. Add onion and carrot; simmer 20 minutes. Add cheese; heat and stir until melted and blended. Add milk and beer; reduce heat to low. Add parsley; heat another 5 minutes. Season to taste with salt and white pepper. Garnish with additional parsley, if desired.

Garden Patch Meatball Soup

Makes 4 servings

2 medium potatoes, peeled
   and cubed
2 medium carrots, peeled
   and sliced
1 medium onion, chopped
4 medium celery stalks with
   tops, coarsely chopped
1 can (16 ounces) tomatoes
2 teaspoons salt
1 teaspoon pepper
1 bay leaf
1 pound lean ground round
1 egg
¼ cup chopped fresh parsley

In a large saucepan, stir together potatoes, carrots, onion, celery, tomatoes, salt, pepper, bay leaf, and 3 cups water. Cover; simmer 30 minutes. While soup simmers, mix together beef, egg, and parsley. Shape into 1-inch balls. Add to soup. Simmer, covered, 15 minutes longer or until meatballs are tender.

Savory Pork Soup

Makes 12 servings

2 pounds boneless pork
   shoulder, cut into 1-inch
   cubes
¼ cup flour
¼ cup vegetable oil
1 bunch green onions, sliced
2 cloves garlic, minced
2 cans (16 ounces each)
   tomatoes
2 cans (10½ ounces each)
   condensed beef broth
1 jar (16 ounces) small boiled
   onions, drained
1 can (6 ounces) vegetable
   juice cocktail
½ cup water
3 stalks celery, sliced into
   1-inch pieces
2 medium yellow squash, sliced
1 bay leaf
2 tablespoons chopped fresh
   parsley
1 teaspoon salt
½ teaspoon seasoned pepper

Dredge pork cubes in flour to coat. In a Dutch oven, heat oil. Brown cubes on all sides in hot oil. Add green onions and garlic; sauté over medium-high heat for one minute, stirring constantly. Add remaining ingredients; bring to a boil. Reduce heat. Cover; simmer for 1 to 1½ hours, stirring occasionally.

SALADS

Crisp Vegetable Medley

Makes 8 servings

2 cups sliced cauliflower
flowerets
2 carrots, cut in julienne strips
1 green pepper, cut in julienne
strips
1 cucumber, cut in rounds
1 cup frozen peas, thawed
½ cup wine vinegar
½ cup olive oil
1 tablespoon sugar
1 teaspoon salt
½ teaspoon oregano
½ teaspoon basil
¼ teaspoon pepper
Cherry tomatoes, stuffed
olives, chopped fresh parsley,
and sunflower seeds as
desired, for garnish

In a serving bowl, place cauliflower, carrots, green pepper, cucumber, and peas. In a small bowl, place vinegar, oil, and seasonings; blend well. Pour over vegetables; toss vegetables to mix. Refrigerate, covered, at least 4 hours; stir occasionally. Just before serving, garnish with cherry tomatoes, olives, parsley, and sunflower seeds.

Eggnog Holiday Salad

Makes 6 to 8 servings

1 can (16 ounces) fruit cocktail,
drained; reserve juice
2 envelopes unflavored gelatin
1 can (11 ounces) mandarin
oranges, drained; cut in
halves
1 cup flaked coconut
2½ cups eggnog
½ cup maraschino cherries, cut
in halves; divided
Dash nutmeg

In a medium saucepan, place reserved juice; sprinkle with gelatin. Heat mixture over low heat, stirring constantly, until gelatin dissolves and mixture is clear. Stir in oranges, coconut, eggnog, ¼ cup cherries, and nutmeg. Turn into a lightly oiled 5-cup mold. Chill until firm. Unmold onto a lettuce-lined serving plate. Garnish with remaining cherries.

Colorful Garden Salad _____

Makes 4 servings

  1 bunch leaf lettuce
  2 carrots, sliced in rounds
  4 radishes, sliced
  1 small onion, sliced
  4 tomatoes, cut into wedges
  1 small cucumber, sliced
    Yogurt Dressing

Line a salad bowl with lettuce. In a separate bowl, stir remaining vegetables to mix. Place in lettuce-lined bowl. Spoon yogurt dressing over all. Garnish as desired.

Yogurt Dressing

Makes 1½ cups

  8 ounces plain yogurt
  ½ cup mayonnaise
  1 tablespoon lemon juice
  1 teaspoon chopped onion
    Dash garlic salt

In a small bowl, blend all ingredients.

Cranberry Apple Salad _____

Makes 4 to 6 servings

  1 tablespoon lemon juice
  2 large apples, unpeeled, cut
    into bite-size pieces
  1 large carrot, grated
  ½ cup currants or raisins
  ½ cup chopped walnuts
  ½ cup whole berry cranberry or
    cranberry-raspberry sauce
  1 teaspoon grated orange peel

Sprinkle lemon juice over apples; toss lightly. Add carrots, currants, and walnuts. Stir in cranberry sauce and orange peel. Chill at least 1 hour. Serve in individual lettuce cups.

Spiced Peaches _____

3½ cups peach halves
  1 tablespoon vinegar
  1 teaspoon whole cloves
  ½ teaspoon nutmeg
    Dark pitted cherries

In a saucepan, combine all ingredients. Bring to a boil, reduce heat, and simmer 5 minutes. Chill. To serve, arrange drained peaches on leaf lettuce; top with cherries.

Salads

Dilled Pea Salad

Makes 6 servings

1 cup sour cream
½ cup chopped dillweed *or* chives
½ to 1 teaspoon curry powder
Salt and pepper to taste
1 can (16 ounces) tiny peas, drained

In a small bowl, combine sour cream, dillweed, curry, salt, and pepper; blend well. Gently stir in peas. Transfer to a serving bowl; chill. Garnish with dill sprigs or chives.

Christmas Cranberry Salad

Makes 6 to 8 servings

1 pound fresh cranberries, coarsely chopped
1 can (20 ounces) crushed pineapple
1½ cups sugar
1 package (16 ounces) miniature marshmallows
1 cup whipping cream

In a mixing bowl, stir together cranberries, pineapple, and sugar; set aside. Rinse marshmallows with cold water; drain thoroughly. In a small bowl, whip cream until stiff. Fold marshmallows into whipped cream. Fold whipped cream and marshmallows into cranberry mixture. Serve on individual lettuce cups.

Chicken and Rice Salad

Makes 12 servings

5 cups cooked chicken, cut in chunks
2 tablespoons vegetable oil
2 tablespoons orange juice
2 tablespoons vinegar
1 teaspoon salt
3 cups cooked long grain rice
1½ cups green grapes
1½ cups thinly sliced celery
1 can (13½ ounces) pineapple tidbits, drained
1 can (11 ounces) mandarin oranges, drained
1 cup slivered almonds, toasted
1½ cups mayonnaise

In a mixing bowl, combine chicken, oil, orange juice, vinegar, and salt; toss lightly to mix. Set aside. In a large bowl, combine rice, grapes, celery, pineapple, oranges, and half of the almonds. Stir in mayonnaise. Add chicken mixture; blend well. Sprinkle with remaining almonds.

Copper Pennies Salad

Makes 8 servings

2 pounds carrots, peeled, sliced,
  and cooked until tender-crisp
1 green pepper, diced
1 medium onion, diced
1 can (10¾ ounces) condensed
  cream of tomato soup
½ cup vegetable oil
¾ cup vinegar
1 cup sugar
1 teaspoon Worcestershire
  sauce
Salt and pepper to taste

In heatproof serving dish or in a medium saucepan, layer carrots, green pepper, and onion. In a bowl, combine soup, oil, vinegar, sugar, Worcestershire sauce, salt, and pepper; blend well. Pour over vegetables. Cook over medium heat until green pepper and onion are tender. Remove from heat; let cool to room temperature. Cover; refrigerate until well chilled.

Cherry Ring Mold

Makes 6 to 8 servings

1 package (6 ounces) cherry-
  flavored gelatin
2 cups boiling water
1½ cups cold water
2 packages (3 ounces *each*)
  cream cheese, softened
½ cup finely chopped walnuts
1 can (16 ounces) pitted dark
  sweet cherries, drained

In a medium bowl, dissolve gelatin in boiling water. Stir in cold water. Chill until slightly thickened. Mix together cream cheese and nuts. Roll into 1½ inch balls; set aside. Spoon 3 to 4 tablespoons thickened gelatin into a lightly oiled ring mold. Arrange half of the cheese balls and half of the cherries alternately in the bottom of the mold. Chill for 20 minutes. Spoon ½ cup gelatin into mold. Refrigerate 20 minutes. Arrange remaining cheese balls and cherries over gelatin layer. Spoon on remaining gelatin. Cover and chill until firm.

Three Bean Apple Salad

Makes 8 servings

2 medium apples, diced
2 cups canned green beans
2 cups canned wax beans
2 cups canned garbanzo beans
¼ cup chopped green onion
¼ cup diagonally-sliced celery
¼ cup Italian dressing
½ cup sliced radishes

In a serving bowl, combine all ingredients except radishes; mix well. Refrigerate at least 4 hours to blend flavors. Just before serving, add radishes; toss.

MAIN DISHES

Cornish Game Hens with Orange Sherry Glaze _____

Makes 4 servings

4 Cornish game hens
¼ cup butter
½ cup chopped onion
½ cup chopped green pepper
2 tablespoons chopped fresh parsley
½ teaspoon thyme
Salt and pepper to taste
3 cups cooked white *or* brown rice
Orange Sherry Glaze

Clean hens inside and out; pat dry. In a skillet, melt butter. Sauté onion and green pepper until onion is golden. Stir sautéed vegetables, parsley, thyme, salt, and pepper into rice. Stuff birds with rice mixture; truss. Place birds breast side up in a roasting pan. Roast, uncovered, 30 minutes. Brush with Orange Sherry Glaze. Bake an additional 30 minutes, basting frequently.

Orange Sherry Glaze

⅓ cup sugar
1 tablespoon cornstarch
¼ teaspoon orange peel
¼ teaspoon lemon peel
1 cup orange juice
¼ cup sherry

In a saucepan, stir together all ingredients. Bring to a boil over medium heat, stirring constantly. Reduce heat; simmer 2 minutes or until glaze thickens.

Pheasant in Cream _____

Makes 4 servings

1 pheasant (2½ to 3 pounds), quartered
1 can (10½ ounces) condensed cream of mushroom soup
½ cup sour cream
1 can (4 ounces) sliced mushrooms, drained
¼ cup grated Parmesan cheese
¼ cup chopped onion

Preheat oven to 350° F. Place pheasant, skin side up, on a rack in a 9 x 13-inch baking pan. In a medium bowl, stir together soup, sour cream, mushrooms, cheese, and onion; pour over pheasant. Bake 1½ to 2 hours or until pheasant is tender. Baste occasionally with sauce.

Cornish Game Hens with Orange Sherry Glaze

Main Dishes

Wild Duck with Apple Stuffing

Makes 6 servings

6 cups croutons
1 cup cubed, unpeeled apple
½ cup raisins
¾ cup butter *or* margarine, melted
2 teaspoons salt
½ teaspoon pepper
¼ teaspoon cinnamon
⅛ teaspoon ground ginger
3 ducks

Preheat oven to 450° F. In a mixing bowl, stir together all ingredients, except ducks. Stuff the ducks; truss. Place ducks breast side up on a rack in a roasting pan. Roast, uncovered, for 15 minutes. Reduce heat to 325° F. Lightly cover ducks with foil. Roast, allowing about 20 minutes per pound to reach an internal temperature of 190° F.

Chicken and Yellow Rice

Makes 6 servings

6 tablespoons olive oil
6 chicken breasts, halved
4 medium onions, chopped
3 medium green peppers, diced
7 large garlic cloves, minced
3 cups uncooked long grain rice
6 cups chicken broth
1 teaspoon turmeric
4 bay leaves
2 teaspoons salt
2 cups frozen peas, thawed
2 pimientos, cut in strips
¼ cup chopped fresh parsley

Preheat oven to 350° F. In a large skillet, heat oil. Add chicken pieces and sauté until golden on both sides. Remove chicken. Add onions, green peppers, and garlic; sauté until onions are soft. Stir rice into vegetables. Add broth and seasonings; bring to a boil. Pour mixture into a large casserole. Arrange chicken pieces on top; cover with foil and bake for 50 minutes. Open foil; sprinkle peas around edge of casserole. Cover and bake 10 minutes longer. Garnish with pimientos and parsley.

Celestial Chicken

Makes 4 servings

⅓ cup flour
1½ teaspoons salt
¼ teaspoon paprika
1 broiler-fryer, cut up
¼ cup vegetable oil
½ cup chopped onion
½ cup dry sherry
¼ cup water
½ cup sour cream
¼ cup mayonnaise
2 tablespoons chopped fresh parsley

In a paper bag, combine flour, salt, paprika, and pepper. Add chicken pieces, a few at a time; shake to coat. Heat oil in a heavy skillet. Add chicken; brown on all sides. Add onion, sherry, and water. Cover; simmer 1 hour or until chicken is tender. Transfer chicken to a hot platter; keep warm. Blend sour cream and mayonnaise into pan juices. Add parsley. Heat through but do not boil. Pour over chicken.

Pork Roast with Herb Stuffing

Makes 10 to 14 servings

1 tablespoon lemon-pepper seasoning
1 teaspoon tarragon
1 teaspoon salt
6 to 8 pound bone-in pork center loin roast
Herb Stuffing
¼ cup honey
1 tablespoon lemon juice
Fresh tarragon sprigs, optional
Lemon slices, optional

Preheat oven to 350° F. In a small bowl, stir together lemon-pepper seasoning, tarragon, and salt. Rub seasonings into roast. Cut slits about 2 inches deep between ribs of roast, without cutting through the opposite side. Pack stuffing into slits. Place roast on rack in a shallow roasting pan. Insert meat thermometer in thickest part of roast, not touching bone or fat. Place a piece of aluminum foil loosely over top of roast just to cover stuffing, making a slit in foil to accommodate meat thermometer. Bake for 30 to 35 minutes per pound or until meat thermometer registers 165°-170° F. Combine honey and lemon juice; brush over roast and stuffing 15 minutes before end of cooking time.

Let roast stand for 15 to 20 minutes before carving to allow juices to set. Garnish with fresh tarragon sprigs and lemon slices, if desired.

Herb Stuffing

Makes 4 cups

½ cup butter *or* margarine
1 bunch green onions with tops, chopped
1 clove garlic, minced
½ cup sliced fresh mushrooms
1 package (8 ounces) herb-seasoned stuffing
1 tablespoon fresh chopped parsley
1 teaspoon lemon-pepper seasoning
½ teaspoon tarragon
½ teaspoon salt
1 egg, beaten
½ cup dry sherry
2 tablespoons lemon juice

In a large skillet over low heat, melt butter. Add onions and garlic; cook over medium-high heat for 3 to 5 minutes. Add mushrooms; continue to cook for 2 to 3 minutes, stirring occasionally. Combine remaining ingredients in a large bowl. Add cooked mixture and toss gently to mix.

Roast Venison

Makes 8 to 10 servings

2½ cups dry red wine
½ cup apple cider
3 bay leaves
4 whole peppercorns
1 venison roast (6 pounds)
¼ cup butter *or* margarine
Sour Cream Gravy

In a shallow dish, combine first 4 ingredients. Place venison in marinade; cover and chill at least 8 hours, turning occasionally. Preheat oven to 350° F. Place meat on a rack in a roasting pan, fat side up. In a small saucepan, melt butter; stir in 1 cup marinade. Insert meat thermometer in thickest part of meat, not touching bone or fat. Place meat in the oven and roast about three hours, allowing 25 minutes per pound for medium-rare. Baste occasionally with marinade mixture. Serve with Sour Cream Gravy.

Sour Cream Gravy

Makes 6 to 8 servings

1½ tablespoons flour
½ teaspoon salt
¾ cup drippings from roast
½ cup dry red wine
1 cup sour cream

In a 1½-quart saucepan, mix flour and salt. Gradually add drippings, stirring until smooth. Add wine. Stir over medium heat until thickened. Reduce heat to low. Stir in sour cream; heat to serving temperature.

Baked Ham with Peach or Cherry Glaze

1 fully cooked boneless ham (6 to 7 pounds)
Peach Glaze *or* 1 can (21 ounces) cherry pie filling

Preheat oven to 325° F. Place ham on a rack in a shallow pan. Bake 2 hours or to an internal temperature of 140° F. Spoon fat from baking pan. Spoon Peach Glaze or cherry pie filling over ham. Use wooden picks to secure cherries. Bake an additional 30 minutes, basting occasionally with glaze or pie filling.

Peach Glaze

1 can (12 ounces) peach nectar
2 teaspoons Worcestershire sauce
2 tablespoons brown sugar

In a small bowl, combine all ingredients; blend well.

Baked Ham with Peach Glaze
Spiced Peaches, 18
Lemony Green Beans and Carrots, 41
Cranberry Pie, 59

Main Dishes

Crown Roast of Lamb with Sesame Rice

1 crown roast of lamb
Sesame Rice
Parsley
Pimiento

Preheat oven to 450° F. Cover ends of bones with aluminum foil. Place meat in the oven; immediately reduce temperature to 350° F. Roast until the meat reaches an internal temperature of 160°-165° F. for rare; or 175° F. for well-done. Plan for 30 minutes per pound for well-done. Remove roast from oven 45 minutes before end of cooking time. Fill with Sesame Rice. Return to oven to finish roasting. When roast is done, remove foil. Garnish with parsley and pimiento.

Sesame Rice

4 cups cooked long grain rice
(2 cups uncooked)
1 can (15 ounces) garbanzos, drained
1 can (8¾ ounces) whole kernel corn
1 tablespoon sesame seed
1 tablespoon lemon juice
Salt and pepper to taste
Chopped fresh parsley, optional

In a mixing bowl, stir together all ingredients.

Veal Tarragon

Makes 6 to 8 servings

2½ pounds veal steak
Salt, pepper, and flour
½ cup butter *or* margarine
½ teaspoon tarragon
Juice of 1 lemon
¼ cup dry sherry
1 cup sour cream

Pound steak to ⅛-inch thickness. Cut into serving pieces. On a breadboard, stir together salt, pepper, and flour. Dredge steaks with flour mixture. In a large skillet, melt butter. Brown steaks on both sides. Transfer steaks to a serving platter; keep warm. In the same skillet at low temperature, mix tarragon, lemon juice, and sherry. Stir to loosen cooked particles. Blend in sour cream. Spoon sauce over veal.

Chateaubriand

Makes 4 servings

2 pounds center portion of beef
  tenderloin
Salt and pepper to taste
Béarnaise Sauce
Sautéed mushrooms

Preheat broiler. Place steak on a rack 5 inches from heat source. Broil 15 minutes. Season with salt and pepper, turn; broil second side 10 to 15 minutes. Season steak with salt and pepper; carve in diagonal slices. Serve with Béarnaise Sauce and mushrooms.

Béarnaise Sauce

½ cup dry white wine
2 tablespoons tarragon vinegar
2 small green onions, chopped
2 sprigs parsley, chopped
¼ teaspoon coarsely ground
  black pepper
3 egg yolks, beaten
½ cup butter, melted
2 teaspoons lemon juice
¼ teaspoon salt
  Dash cayenne pepper

In the top of a double boiler, combine wine, vinegar, onions, parsley, and black pepper. Cook until mixture is reduced to about ⅓ cup. Cool and add to beaten egg yolks, stirring to blend. Return mixture to pan and cook over hot (not boiling) water, stirring constantly until thickened. Remove from hot water. Gradually add butter, beating until smooth. Stir in lemon juice, salt, and cayenne pepper.

Spiced Orange Pot Roast

Makes 6 to 8 servings

1 tablespoon bacon drippings
4 to 5 pounds beef chuck roast
½ cup minced onion
1 clove garlic, minced
1 can (8 ounces) tomato sauce
2 cups orange sections
2 tablespoons sugar
1 tablespoon grated orange
  peel
1½ teaspoons salt
½ teaspoon nutmeg
½ teaspoon cinnamon
¼ teaspoon cloves
  Dash pepper
  Orange slices, optional
  Watercress or parsley,
  optional

In a heavy skillet or Dutch oven, heat drippings. Brown meat slowly on all sides. Add onion and garlic. Cover; simmer gently 20 minutes. Add tomato sauce, orange sections, sugar, and grated orange peel to skillet. Sprinkle meat with salt and spices. Cover; simmer gently until meat is tender, about 2 hours. Garnish with orange slices and watercress or parsley.

"Friends, relatives come to call,
Feasting, sharing,
Laughing at tales retold."
Joan C. Callahan

CASSEROLES

Beef and Noodle Casserole

Makes two 1-quart casseroles

1½ pounds ground beef
  1 medium onion, chopped
  1 medium green pepper, chopped
 ⅓ cup chopped celery
  1 clove garlic, minced
  1 can (14½ ounces) tomatoes, undrained
  1 can (6 ounces) tomato paste
  1 bay leaf
  1 tablespoon chopped fresh parsley
  1 teaspoon salt
 ½ teaspoon pepper
 ½ teaspoon paprika
  8 ounces noodles or macaroni
  2 tablespoons butter or margarine
  2 tablespoons flour
1½ cups milk
 ¼ cup chopped green onion
  2 egg yolks
  1 cup shredded Monterey Jack cheese
  1 package (10 ounces) frozen green peas, thawed and drained
  2 tablespoons Parmesan cheese
    Cherry tomatoes
    Chopped fresh parsley

In a skillet over medium-high heat, sauté ground beef until lightly browned. Add onion, green pepper, celery, and garlic; sauté 10 minutes, stirring frequently. Drain fat. Add tomatoes, tomato paste, bay leaf, parsley, salt, pepper, and paprika; stir and bring to a boil. Reduce heat, cover, and simmer about 40 minutes. Cook noodles according to package directions. Drain; set aside. In a heavy saucepan over medium heat, melt butter. Add flour, stirring until smooth. Cook 1 minute, stirring constantly. Gradually add milk, stirring constantly until slightly thickened and bubbly. Stir in green onion; continue to cook 1 minute. Beat egg yolks. Gradually stir about ¼ of the white sauce into egg yolks; return to remaining sauce, stirring constantly. Add Monterey Jack cheese, stirring until the sauce thickens and cheese melts.

Preheat oven to 350° F. Butter two 1-quart casseroles In a mixing bowl, stir pasta and peas together. Add Parmesan cheese; mix gently. Spoon pasta mixture around sides of prepared casseroles. Spoon half of the beef mixture into center of each. Bake one casserole for 20 minutes. To serve, garnish with cherry tomatoes and parsley. Wrap the other casserole and freeze. To bake, thaw overnight in refrigerator. Let stand at room temperature for 15 minutes. Bake at 350° F. for 45 minutes or until hot and bubbly.

Casseroles

Crumb Topped Fish Fillets

Makes 4 to 6 servings

6 green onions, chopped
⅓ cup mushrooms, sliced
2 pounds fish fillets
1 teaspoon salt
½ teaspoon pepper
1 teaspoon marjoram
2 tablespoons dry white wine
2 teaspoons lemon juice
¼ cup Monterey Jack cheese, grated
¼ cup bread crumbs
½ cup butter, melted

Preheat oven to 400° F. Butter a baking dish large enough to hold the fillets in one layer with slight overlapping. Sprinkle the green onions and mushrooms over bottom of the dish. Arrange fillets over the vegetables, covering the thin part of each fillet with the thick part of another to prevent overcooking. Sprinkle fillets with seasonings, wine, and lemon juice. Top with cheese and bread crumbs. Pour butter over all. Wrinkle a piece of waxed paper, wet it, and place lightly over fish. Bake 7 minutes. Remove waxed paper; bake 5 minutes longer.

Boston Baked Scallops

Makes 4 servings

1 pound scallops
2 tablespoons vegetable oil
¼ cup sliced green onion
1 can (10¾ ounces) condensed cream of shrimp soup
⅓ cup half-and-half or milk
1 package (10 ounces) frozen cut asparagus, cooked and drained
1 tablespoon lemon juice
2 cups coarsely broken potato chips
16 whole potato chips

Preheat oven to 400° F. Rinse scallops with cold water to remove any shell particles. In a large skillet, heat oil. Sauté scallops and green onion about 5 minutes or until scallops are tender. Add soup and half-and-half; stir thoroughly. Fold in asparagus and lemon juice. Heat to just below simmering. Sprinkle broken potato chips over bottom of a shallow 1½-quart baking dish. Spoon ½ of scallop mixture evenly over crushed chips. Stand whole potato chips on end around edge of baking dish. Spoon remaining scallop mixture into dish. Bake 10 minutes or until hot and bubbly.

Elegant Fish Turbans

Makes 6 servings

6 fish fillets, ½ inch thick or less, skinned
½ teaspoon salt
¼ teaspoon pepper
Florentine stuffing
¼ cup butter _or_ margarine, melted
Shrimp Sauce
Pimiento strips

Preheat oven to 350° F. Sprinkle fish with salt and pepper; set aside. Prepare Florentine Stuffing. Place approximately ½ cup stuffing on each fillet. Roll fillets around stuffing and secure with wooden picks or skewers. Place turbans in a shallow, well-greased baking dish. Drizzle with margarine. Bake for 25 minutes or until fish flakes easily when tested with a fork. Top with Shrimp Sauce. Garnish with pimiento strips.

Florentine Stuffing

6 ounces onion-garlic croutons
½ cup chopped celery
¼ cup butter _or_ margarine
1 egg, beaten
2 cups chopped fresh _or_ frozen spinach
½ teaspoon salt
¼ teaspoon thyme
⅛ teaspoon pepper

Combine all ingredients; mix thoroughly.

Shrimp Sauce

1 can (10¾ ounces) condensed cream of shrimp soup
¼ cup milk
1 tablespoon dry sherry
Shrimp, cooked and chopped, optional

In a saucepan, place soup, milk, and sherry; blend well. Add additional shrimp if a heartier sauce is desired. Heat through.

Imperial Crab

Makes 4 servings

¼ cup butter
1 cup half-and-half
1 egg, lightly beaten
1 teaspoon lemon juice
1 teaspoon dry mustard
2 teaspoons Worcestershire sauce
Salt and pepper to taste
1 pound crab meat
Cracker crumbs

Preheat oven to 400° F. In top of a double boiler, melt butter. Stir in half-and-half, egg, mustard, lemon juice, Worcestershire sauce, salt, and pepper. Stir in crab meat. Spoon into individual casseroles. Sprinkle cracker crumbs over tops. Bake 30 minutes.

Casseroles

Cheddar Crust Meat Pies

Makes 4 servings

2 eggs
1 can (10¾ ounces) condensed
   cream of mushroom soup
1 can (13 ounces) evaporated
   milk
1 cup cubed cooked chicken
1 cup cubed cooked ham
1 large cooked potato, cut in
   ⅛-inch slices
2 cups frozen mixed vegetables,
   thawed
¼ teaspoon marjoram
   Cheddar Crust
   Milk

Preheat oven to 400° F. Butter four 2-cup casseroles or one 2-quart casserole. In a mixing bowl, beat eggs. Blend in soup and evaporated milk. Stir in chicken, ham, potato slices, mixed vegetables, and marjoram. Pour into casseroles. Roll out Cheddar Crust to fit over casseroles. Cut slits in pastry; brush with milk. Bake 25 minutes or until crust is golden.

Cheddar Crust

Makes crust for four 2-cup casseroles

1½ cups flour
   Dash salt
½ cup shortening
1½ cups lightly packed shredded
   Cheddar cheese
4 to 6 tablespoons ice water

In a mixing bowl, stir together flour and salt. Cut in shortening until mixture resembles coarse crumbs. Stir in cheese. Sprinkle with 2 tablespoons water; gently toss with a fork. Continue to add water and toss until dough is moistened and holds together. Form into 4 balls of dough.

Cheesy Turkey Casserole

Makes 6 to 8 servings

2 cups frozen green beans
4 tablespoons butter or
   margarine
¼ cup finely chopped onion
4 tablespoons flour
½ teaspoon salt
1½ cups milk
2 cups chopped cooked turkey
2 hard-cooked eggs, chopped
1 cup shredded Cheddar cheese
2 tablespoons pimiento
1 tablespoon chopped fresh
   parsley
½ cup herb croutons

Preheat oven to 350° F. Butter a 1½-quart casserole. Cook beans according to package directions; drain, reserving ½ cup cooking liquid. In a 2-quart saucepan, melt butter; sauté onion. Stir in flour and salt until blended. Remove from heat; stir in milk and reserved ½ cup liquid. Bring to a boil, stirring constantly. Boil and stir 1 minute. Remove from heat; stir in turkey, eggs, cheese, pimiento, and parsley. Place beans in prepared casserole; cover with sauce. Sprinkle croutons over top. Bake for 20 to 25 minutes.

Cheddar Crust Meat Pies

Casseroles

Baked Stuffed Rigatoni

Makes 8 to 10 servings

16 ounces rigatoni
4 pounds Italian sausage
¾ cup chopped onion
2 cloves garlic, minced
2 eggs, beaten
½ cup dry bread crumbs
3 tablespoons chopped fresh
  parsley
  Salt and pepper
3 cans (15 ounces *each*) tomato
  sauce
  Parmesan cheese

Preheat oven to 350° F. Butter a 9 x 13-inch baking pan and a 9 x 9-inch baking pan. Cook rigatoni according to package directions. Drain; rinse with cold water. Spread on cookie sheets to separate. In a skillet, sauté sausage until lightly browned. Add onion and garlic; sauté until onion is tender. Remove from heat; cool slightly. Blend in eggs, bread crumbs, and parsley. Season to taste with salt and pepper. Stuff rigatoni with meat mixture. Place in prepared pans. Pour ⅔ of the tomato sauce over the rigatoni. Bake 15 minutes. Spoon remaining sauce over top; bake an additional 15 minutes. Sprinkle with Parmesan cheese.

Veal Marengo

Makes 8 servings

3 tablespoons olive oil
4 pounds boneless veal, cut in
  1-inch cubes
1 clove garlic, minced
1 pound mushrooms, sliced
20 small white onions, peeled
3 tablespoons flour
2½ teaspoons salt
½ teaspoon pepper
1 can (16 ounces) tomatoes
1 cup dry white wine
2 cups chicken broth
1 stalk celery, chopped
4 sprigs parsley
¼ teaspoon thyme
1 bay leaf

Preheat oven to 325° F. In a large skillet, heat oil. Add veal and garlic; sauté until veal is browned. Transfer veal to a large casserole. In the same skillet, brown mushrooms and onions. Transfer to casserole. Stir flour, salt, and pepper into drippings in skillet. Add tomatoes, wine, and broth, mixing well. Add celery, parsley, thyme, and bay leaf. Simmer and stir until sauce thickens and celery is tender. Pour mixture over meat. Bake, covered, for 1 hour and 15 minutes. Remove bay leaf. Serve at once, or, for even better flavor, freeze. Thaw; reheat in covered casserole at 350° F. for 45 minutes. Serve with noodles.

Vegetarian Moussaka

1 eggplant (1 to 1¼ pounds)
¼ cup butter *or* margarine, melted
2 tablespoons vegetable oil
1 medium onion, chopped
1 tablespoon flour
¼ pound mushrooms, sliced
1 cup pitted ripe olives, halved
1 can (8 ounces) tomato sauce
½ cup tomato puree
1½ teaspoons basil
1½ teaspoons oregano
2 tablespoons dry bread crumbs
3 medium potatoes, cooked, peeled, and sliced
Cheese sauce

Preheat oven to 400° F. Cut eggplant in ¼-inch slices and halve each slice. Place eggplant pieces in a shallow baking dish and brush with half the melted butter. Turn and brush other side with remaining butter. Bake 20 minutes or until eggplant is tender. In a large skillet, heat oil. Sauté onion until soft. Stir in flour. Add mushrooms, olives, tomato sauce, tomato puree, basil, and oregano. Heat, stirring, until sauce thickens and comes to a boil. Layer half the eggplant in a 2-quart casserole. Sprinkle with half the bread crumbs; add half the olive sauce. Top with potato slices, remaining eggplant, bread crumbs and olive sauce. Top with Cheese Sauce. Bake 40 minutes, or until heated through.

Cheese Sauce

2 tablespoons butter
2 tablespoons flour
1¼ cups milk
¾ cup grated Cheddar cheese
Salt and pepper to taste

In a saucepan, melt butter. Blend in flour. Gradually add milk, stirring to blend. Cook, stirring constantly, over medium heat until sauce thickens and just begins to bubble. Stir in cheese, salt, and pepper. Heat and stir until sauce is smooth.

Yam Shepherd's Pie

Makes 6 servings

2 pounds (3 large) yams, pared and cut into 2-inch pieces
3 tablespoons butter *or* margarine
¾ cup sliced fresh mushrooms
1 large onion, chopped
2 stalks celery, chopped
2 cups cooked turkey, chopped
½ cup milk
1 teaspoon salt
½ teaspoon thyme
¼ teaspoon nutmeg
¼ cup chopped walnuts

Preheat oven to 400° F. Butter a 1½-quart casserole. In a large saucepan, simmer yams in slightly salted water until tender, about 30 minutes; drain. Mash yams and set aside. In a large skillet, melt butter. Sauté mushrooms, onion, and celery until tender. Add turkey, milk, salt, thyme, and nutmeg; mix well. Blend in 1 cup mashed yams. Spoon turkey mixture into prepared casserole. Spread remaining yams over turkey mixture. Sprinkle with walnuts. Bake for 30 minutes. Place under broiler 1 minute to brown top slightly before serving.

SIDE DISHES

Savory Blackeyed Peas

Makes 6 servings

2 cups water
20 ounces frozen blackeyed
  peas
2 tablespoons vegetable oil
1½ cups chopped onion
1 clove garlic, minced
8 ounces tomato sauce
1 teaspoon oregano
1 teaspoon basil
  Salt and pepper to taste
1 tablespoon lemon juice

In a large saucepan, bring water to a boil. Add frozen peas; bring to a boil. Reduce heat, cover, and simmer gently for 15 minutes. Drain, reserving ¾ cup cooking liquid; set aside. In a heavy skillet, heat oil. Sauté onion and garlic until onion is golden. Stir in tomato sauce, oregano, basil, salt, and pepper. Simmer 5 minutes. Stir in peas, cooking liquid, and lemon juice. Cover; simmer, stirring often, about 30 minutes or until sauce is thick.

Carolina Yam Patties

Makes 8 servings

3 cups hot mashed yams
3 tablespoons butter *or*
  margarine
1 teaspoon salt
⅛ teaspoon pepper
2 tablespoons sugar
1 cup cornflakes, crushed

Preheat oven to 350° F. In a bowl, combine yams, butter, salt, pepper, and sugar; blend well. Shape mixture into 8 patties. Roll in crushed cornflakes. Bake on a buttered baking sheet for 15 minutes or until lightly browned. Serve with pork, ham, or poultry.

Red Cabbage with Raisins

Makes 6 servings

1 head red cabbage, shredded
¼ cup raisins
½ cup water
½ cup apple juice
2 tablespoons light brown
  sugar
1½ teaspoons salt
  Juice of 1 lemon

In a large skillet, stir together all ingredients. Cover; simmer until cabbage is tender and most of the liquid has evaporated.

Side Dishes

Party Peas

Makes 6 servings

2 slices bacon, cut in ½-inch
  pieces
1 stalk celery, sliced
2 green onions, sliced
1 cup finely shredded spinach
  or lettuce
1 teaspoon flour
⅓ cup beef or chicken broth
1 can (16 ounces) peas, drained
½ teaspoon seasoned salt
¼ cup slivered almonds, toasted

In a small skillet, cook bacon until almost crisp. Add celery and onions. Sauté until bacon is crisp, stirring often. Add spinach. Cover; simmer for 5 minutes. Stir in flour; blend in broth. Cook, stirring constantly, until thickened. Add peas, salt, and almonds; toss lightly. Heat to serving temperature.

Peanut Stuffed Squash

Makes 4 servings

2 acorn squash
2 tablespoons butter
2 cups minced baked ham
2 tablespoons chopped onion
1 tablespoon packed light
  brown sugar
1 tablespoon grated orange
  peel
¼ cup orange juice
1 teaspoon salt
1 cup peanuts, chopped
1½ tablespoons butter, melted
¼ cup chopped parsley

Halve squash and remove seeds. Place squash, cut sides down, on a greased baking sheet. Bake at 350° F. for 45 minutes or until tender. Scoop out pulp, leaving a thin shell. Place pulp in a mixing bowl. In a small skillet, melt 2 tablespoons butter. Lightly brown ham and onion. Stir into squash pulp. Add brown sugar, orange peel, juice, salt, and peanuts. Fill shells with squash mixture. Drizzle with melted butter. Bake at 350° F. for 20 to 30 minutes or until heated through. Garnish with parsley.

Bavarian Wax Beans

Makes 4 servings

4 slices bacon, cut in ½-inch
  pieces
2 green onions, sliced
1 stalk celery, diagonally sliced
1 can (16 ounces) wax beans,
  drained
⅓ cup white wine vinegar
¾ teaspoon salt
3 tablespoons sugar
1 tablespoon diced pimiento

In a small skillet, cook bacon until almost crisp. Drain drippings, reserving about 2 tablespoons in skillet. Add onions and celery. Sauté until bacon is crisp. Stir in beans, vinegar, salt, and sugar. Heat through. Garnish with pimiento.

Lemony Green Beans and Carrots

Makes 6 servings

1 pound green beans, ends
  trimmed
½ pound carrots, sliced
  diagonally
4 tablespoons butter
2 teaspoons lemon juice

In a large skillet, bring 1 inch of water to a boil. Add vegetables. Cover, reduce heat, and simmer just until tender, about 7 minutes. In a saucepan, melt butter; blend in lemon juice. Arrange vegetables on a serving platter. Drizzle with lemon butter.

Louisiana Rice Dressing

Makes 8 servings

1 tablespoon bacon drippings
1 tablespoon flour
1 onion, chopped
2 stalks celery, chopped
½ green pepper, chopped
2 cloves garlic, minced
3 green onions, chopped
1 can (4 ounces) mushrooms
  drained; reserve liquid
1 teaspoon instant chicken
  bouillon
⅛ teaspoon hot pepper sauce
1 teaspoon Worcestershire
  sauce
1 package long grain and wild
  rice, cooked according to
  package directions
¾ pound pork sausage, cooked,
  drained, and crumbled

Preheat oven to 325° F. In a large skillet, combine bacon drippings and flour. Cook over medium heat, stirring constantly until flour is browned. Stir in onion, celery, green pepper, garlic, mushrooms, and green onions. Combine mushroom liquid with enough water to equal 1½ cups. Add bouillon granules; stir to dissolve. Stir in hot pepper sauce and Worcestershire sauce. Combine vegetable mixture, rice, and sausage in a large baking dish; mix well. Pour seasoned bouillon over rice mixture. Bake for 30 minutes or until heated through.

Baked Rice with Vermicelli

Makes 12 servings

2 cups uncooked long grain rice
2 beef bouillon cubes
½ cup butter or margarine
1 large onion, chopped
1 green pepper, chopped
1 cup vermicelli, broken into
  1-inch pieces
1½ teaspoons curry powder
½ teaspoon salt
1 can (10½ ounces) condensed
  consommé

Preheat oven to 300° F. Butter a 3-quart casserole. Cook rice according to package directions, adding bouillon cubes to water. In a large skillet, melt butter. Sauté onion, green pepper, and vermicelli in butter until onion is golden and vermicelli is light brown. Stir in cooked rice, seasonings, and undiluted consommé. Spoon into prepared casserole. Cover; bake 30 minutes.

Florentine Scalloped Potatoes

Makes 6 servings

1 can (10¾ ounces) condensed
  Cheddar cheese soup
1 can (16 ounces) tomatoes,
  drained and chopped
1 package (10 ounces) frozen
  chopped spinach, thawed
½ cup sliced onion
1 tablespoon chopped fresh
  parsley
½ teaspoon lemon juice
½ teaspoon marjoram
1 clove garlic, minced
  Dash pepper
2 cups shredded Swiss cheese,
  divided
4 cups thinly sliced potatoes

Preheat oven to 375° F. Butter a 2-quart casserole. In a mixing bowl, stir together all ingredients except ½ cup cheese and the sliced potatoes. In the prepared casserole, layer sauce alternately with potatoes, beginning and ending with sauce. Cover; bake 1 hour and 10 minutes. Uncover; sprinkle with reserved cheese. Bake an additional 15 minutes.

Party Potatoes

Makes 6 servings

¼ cup butter *or* margarine
1 cup shredded Cheddar cheese,
  lightly packed
1½ cups sour cream
⅓ cup chopped green onions
1 teaspoon salt
¼ teaspoon pepper
6 medium potatoes, baked
  Paprika

Preheat oven to 325° F. In a saucepan, melt butter. Add cheese; heat, stirring constantly, until cheese is melted. Add sour cream, green onions, salt, and pepper; mix well. Pour into a 2-quart casserole. Scoop potatoes from skins and add directly to casserole without mashing. Toss potatoes in sour cream mixture just enough to coat potatoes. Sprinkle paprika over all. Bake for about 45 minutes or until potatoes are heated through.

Orange Glazed Beets

Makes 4 to 5 servings

1 can (16 ounces) sliced beets
1 tablespoon butter *or*
  margarine
2 teaspoons flour
2 tablespoons brown sugar
½ cup orange juice

In a small saucepan, place beets and their liquid. Heat through. In a separate small saucepan, melt butter. Stir in flour, brown sugar, and orange juice. Cook, stirring constantly until thickened. Drain beets. Stir into sauce and serve.

BRUNCH

Hot Fruit Compote

Makes 20 servings

12 ounces pitted prunes
6 ounces dried apricots
1 can (20 ounces) pineapple
  chunks
1 can (16 ounces) mandarin
  oranges
1 can (21 ounces) cherry pie
  filling
¾ cup white wine

Preheat oven to 300° F. In a casserole, mix all ingredients together. Bake, uncovered, for 45 minutes.

Bran Muffins

Makes 12 muffins

3 cups all-bran cereal
1 cup boiling water
½ cup butter *or* margarine
1½ cups sugar
2 eggs, beaten
2 cups buttermilk
2½ cups flour
2½ teaspoons baking soda
¼ teaspoon salt
⅓ cup currants, optional

Preheat oven to 400° F. Butter one muffin tin. In a medium bowl, place bran cereal; pour in boiling water. Set aside. In a mixing bowl, cream butter and sugar until well blended. Add eggs and buttermilk. Add flour, soda, and salt to shortening mixture. Fold in bran. Add currants, if desired. Do not beat. Spoon gently into muffin cups. Bake for 15 to 18 minutes.

Fruited Fluffy Yogurt

Makes 6 servings

1 package (3 ounces) fruit
  gelatin
1 cup fruit juice
1 cup plain yogurt
2 cups fruit, fresh *or* canned

Prepare fruit gelatin according to package directions, substituting 1 cup fruit juice for 1 cup water. Chill until just beginning to set. Whip with electric beater until fluffy. Blend in yogurt. Stir in fruit. Spoon into dessert dishes or parfait glasses. Chill in the refrigerator until set.

Fancy Scrambled Eggs

Makes 10 servings

Cheese sauce
3 tablespoons butter *or* margarine
1 cup diced Canadian bacon
¼ cup chopped onion
12 eggs, beaten
1 can (3 ounces) mushroom stems and pieces, drained
4 teaspoons butter, melted
2¼ cups soft bread crumbs
⅛ teaspoon paprika

Preheat oven to 350° F. Prepare Cheese Sauce. In a large skillet, melt 3 tablespoons butter. Add Canadian bacon and onion; sauté until onion is tender but not brown. Add eggs and scramble just until set. Fold mushrooms and Cheese Sauce into eggs. Turn into a 12 x 7-inch baking dish. Mix together 4 tablespoons butter, crumbs, and paprika; sprinkle over eggs. Bake uncovered for 30 minutes.

Cheese Sauce

2 tablespoons butter
2 tablespoons flour
½ teaspoon salt
½ teaspoon pepper
2 cups milk
1 cup shredded American cheese

In a saucepan over medium heat, melt butter. Blend in flour, salt, and pepper. Gradually add milk, stirring constantly. Cook, stirring, until bubbly. Add cheese; stir and heat until melted and well blended.

Hash Brown Quiche

Makes 8 servings

24 ounces frozen hash brown potatoes, thawed
⅓ cup butter *or* margarine, melted
1 cup lightly packed shredded Cheddar cheese
1 cup lightly packed shredded Jack cheese
1 cup diced cooked ham
½ cup milk *or* half-and-half
2 eggs
¼ teaspoon seasoned salt

Preheat oven to 425° F. Butter a 9-inch pie pan. Press thawed potatoes between paper towels to absorb excess moisture. Press potatoes firmly into pie pan, trimming to make a neat crust. Brush crust with melted butter. Bake for 20 minutes. Reduce temperature to 350° F. In a mixing bowl, toss cheeses and ham to mix; place in pie crust. In a small bowl, beat milk with eggs and salt. Pour over cheese. Bake at 350° F. until knife inserted near the center comes out clean.

Beaten eggs for scrambled eggs or omelets should be poured into sizzling butter or oil in a hot pan to keep them from sticking. Reduce heat to finish cooking.

Mixed Vegetable Frittata

Makes 3 servings

1 strip bacon, diced
1 small zucchini, coarsely
   shredded
1 green pepper, chopped
1 small onion, chopped
6 eggs, beaten
¼ cup milk
½ teaspoon salt
½ teaspoon pepper
   Butter
   Parsley sprigs
   Tomato wedges

In a large skillet, sauté bacon until translucent. Add zucchini, green pepper, and onion. Sauté until onion is tender and bacon is crisp. In a mixing bowl, combine eggs, milk, salt, and pepper; beat until well blended. Add butter, if needed, to skillet. Pour in egg mixture. Cover and cook over low heat about 10 minutes or until eggs are set. Garnish with parsley and tomato wedges.

Day-Ahead Cheese Soufflé

Makes 6 servings

8 slices white bread
¼ cup butter or margarine
6 eggs, well beaten
   Salt and pepper to taste
2 cups milk
¾ pound sharp Cheddar cheese,
   grated

Cut crusts from bread; cut bread into cubes. In a saucepan, melt butter. In a mixing bowl, stir together melted butter, eggs, salt, and pepper. Blend milk into egg mixture. In an unbuttered casserole, place half of the bread cubes, then half of the grated cheese. Repeat. Pour egg mixture over all. Refrigerate at least 8 hours or overnight. Bake at 350° F. for 1½ hours.

Wheat Germ French Toast

Makes 6 servings

1 egg, beaten
¼ cup milk
¼ cup wheat germ
¼ teaspoon vanilla
6 slices bread
   Cinnamon
   Confectioners' sugar

In a shallow bowl, mix egg, milk, wheat germ, and vanilla. Soak bread in the egg mixture until all the egg mixture is absorbed. On a hot, greased griddle, brown bread on both sides. Sprinkle with cinnamon and confectioners' sugar.

Easy Vegetable Quiche

Makes 6 servings

1 tablespoon butter
1 green pepper, chopped
1 finely chopped onion
1 finely chopped tomato
8 ounces sliced fresh
  mushrooms
1 teaspoon garlic
1 frozen 9-inch pie shell
5 eggs
½ cup milk *or* cream
1 teaspoon oregano
½ teaspoon paprika
4 ounces Monterey Jack cheese,
  shredded

Preheat oven to 350° F. In a large skillet, melt butter. Add green pepper, onion, tomato, mushrooms, and garlic. Sauté until onion is tender. Arrange vegetables in pie shell. In a mixing bowl, stir together eggs, milk, oregano, and paprika; blend well. Pour over vegetables. Top with cheese. Bake for 45 minutes or until eggs are set in center.

Plum Kuchen

Makes 9 servings

½ cup butter *or* margarine
1 cup sugar
1¼ cups flour
½ teaspoon salt
½ teaspoon cinnamon
¼ teaspoon baking powder
1 can (1 pound 4 ounces) plums,
  drained and pitted
1 egg, lightly beaten
1 cup whipping cream

Preheat oven to 375° F. In a large mixing bowl, cream butter and sugar. In a separate bowl, stir together flour, salt, cinnamon, and baking powder. Blend flour and butter mixtures together until crumbly. Set aside ⅓ cup of crumb mixture. Press remaining crumb mixture onto bottom and 1 inch up sides of an ungreased 8 x 8-inch pan. Arrange plums on crust; sprinkle with remaining crumbs. Bake for 15 minutes. Add egg to whipping cream; blend well. Pour over plums. Bake 20 minutes longer or until custard is set. Cool completely before serving.

BREADS

Christmas Stollen _____

Makes 3 large stollen

1½ cups milk
1 cup sugar
1½ teaspoons salt
¾ cup butter
2 packages active dry yeast
1 tablespoon sugar
2 whole eggs
2 egg yolks
3 cups flour

½ teaspoon cardamom
½ cup raisins
½ cup finely chopped candied citron
½ cup sliced candied cherries
2⅔ cups flour

Melted butter
Confectioners' Sugar Icing
Candied fruit
Almonds

In a medium saucepan, scald milk. Add sugar, salt, and butter. Stir; cool to luke-warm. In a small bowl, mix yeast with 1 tablespoon sugar. Add to lukewarm milk mixture; blend well. In a large mixing bowl, beat whole eggs and egg yolks. Add yeast mixture; stir to blend. Add three cups flour; beat until well blended. Cover and let rise in a warm place until doubled in bulk, about 1½ hours.

Punch down dough. Stir in cardamom, raisins, citron, and cherries. Add flour until dough pulls from side of bowl and is no longer sticky to touch. Turn out onto a light-ly floured surface and knead until smooth and satiny. Place in a lightly buttered bowl, turning to butter all sides. Cover and let rise until doubled in bulk, about 1½ hours.

Preheat oven to 350° F. Butter a cookie sheet. Divide dough into thirds. On a floured surface, roll out each piece to an 8 x 10-inch oval. Brush with melted butter. Press a crease down the center of ovals; fold over lengthwise. Place on cookie sheets. Brush with melted butter. Let rise until doubled in bulk, about 45 minutes. Bake about 25 min-utes or until golden brown. Frost with Con-fectioners' Sugar Icing. Decorate with fruit and nuts.

Confectioners' Sugar Icing

1½ cups confectioners' sugar
½ teaspoon vanilla
¼ teaspoon almond extract
Milk

In a small bowl, blend sugar, vanilla, and almond extract, adding enough milk to bring mixture to spreading consistency.

Sesame Potato Twist Loaf ——————

Makes 2 loaves

½ cup butter
½ cup mashed hot cooked
  potatoes or prepared instant
  mashed potatoes
2 tablespoons sugar
2 teaspoons salt
1 cup milk, scalded
2 packages active dry yeast
⅓ cup warm water
5½ cups flour, divided

1 egg white, lightly beaten with
1 tablespoon water
Sesame seeds

In a large mixing bowl, combine butter and potatoes; stir until butter is melted. Add sugar, salt, and milk; stir until mixture is smooth and cooled to lukewarm. In a small bowl, dissolve yeast in warm water; stir into potato mixture. Stir in 3 cups of the flour, beating with a spoon until smooth. Gradually stir in enough of the remaining flour to make a moderately firm dough which does not stick to sides of bowl. Turn out onto a lightly floured board. Knead until smooth and elastic, about 10 minutes, working in only as much additional flour as needed (about 1 cup) to prevent dough from sticking. Place dough in a buttered bowl, turning to butter all sides. Cover and let rise in a warm place until doubled in bulk, about 50 minutes.

Butter two 9 x 5-inch loaf pans. Punch dough down and turn out onto a lightly floured surface. Divide into four parts and roll each part between buttered palms to form a strand about 15 inches long. Spiral-wrap 2 strands together to form a twisted loaf; tuck ends under. Repeat with remaining strands. Place twists in prepared loaf pans. Cover and let rise in a warm place until almost doubled in bulk, about 20 to 30 minutes. Gently brush tops of loaves with egg white; generously sprinkle with sesame seeds. Bake in a 400° F. oven for 10 minutes. Reduce heat to 350° F. and bake for 35 minutes or until golden brown. Turn loaves out to cool on wire racks.

Breads

Onion Rye Bread

Makes 1 large round loaf

    3 cups all-purpose flour
2½ cups rye flour
    ¼ cup brown sugar
    2 packages active dry yeast
    2 teaspoons salt
    1 envelope onion soup mix
1¼ cups water
    1 cup milk
    2 tablespoons butter *or*
        margarine
    ½ teaspoon caraway seed
        Melted butter *or* margarine

In a medium bowl, stir together all-purpose flour and rye flour. In a large bowl, stir together 1½ cups mixed flour, brown sugar, yeast, and salt. In a saucepan, combine onion soup mix, water, milk, 2 tablespoons butter, and caraway seed. Heat, stirring constantly, until lukewarm. Gradually beat liquid mixture into yeast mixture until blended. Gradually stir in enough additional flour (2 to 3 cups) to make a soft dough. Cover and let rise in a warm place until doubled, 40 to 50 minutes.

Preheat oven to 350° F. Butter a 2-quart casserole. Stir dough down. Place in buttered casserole. Brush top with melted butter. Let rise until doubled, 20 to 30 minutes. Bake 50 to 60 minutes. Remove from casserole; brush crust with melted butter. Cool on wire rack.

Dark Pineapple Date Bread

Makes 1 loaf

    2 cups flour
    ¼ cup light brown sugar,
        firmly packed
    1 tablespoon baking powder
    1 teaspoon salt
    1 can (8 ounces) crushed
        pineapple
1¼ cups chopped, pitted dates
    1 cup chopped pecans

    2 eggs
⅔ cup milk
    ¼ cup vegetable oil

Preheat oven to 350° F. Butter an 8 x 4-inch loaf pan. Line pan with waxed paper; grease paper. In a mixing bowl, stir together flour, sugar, baking powder, and salt. Set aside. In a small saucepan, combine pineapple, pineapple liquid, and dates. Cook over low heat, stirring, until liquid is absorbed and mixture is dark and thick. Stir in nuts. Remove from heat; cool 10 minutes.

In a mixing bowl, combine eggs, milk, and oil. Add date mixture; stir until smooth. Add to flour mixture, stirring only until flour is moistened. Pour batter into prepared pan. Bake 60 minutes or until bread tests done. Cover the bread lightly with foil during the last 15 minutes of baking time to prevent excess browning. Cool in the pan on a wire rack.

Elephant Ears

Makes 12 elephant ears

3 egg yolks
1 whole egg
6 tablespoons cold water
1 teaspoon salt
2 cups flour
Cooking oil
Confectioners' sugar

Beat whole eggs and egg yolks until very fluffy, about 8 minutes. Beat in water and salt. Blend in flour, working with hands if necessary. On a well-floured surface, knead the dough briefly until no longer sticky but still soft. Divide dough into 12 equal portions. On a floured surface, roll each portion out to a very thin 8-inch circle. Into a heavy skillet, pour cooking oil to a depth of 1 inch. Heat to 375° F. Gently place one circle of dough at a time in hot oil, frying 10 to 15 seconds per side. Be careful when handling; elephant ears break easily. Remove from oil when golden yellow. Drain on paper towels. Sprinkle with confectioners' sugar.

Hungarian Christmas Bread

Makes 2 loaves

4½ to 5 cups flour, divided
2 packages active dry yeast
½ cup milk
½ cup water
½ cup sugar
¼ cup oil
2 teaspoons salt
2 eggs

1 can (12 ounces) poppy seed filling
1 cup golden raisins
1 egg, room temperature
Poppy seed

In a mixing bowl, stir together 2 cups flour and yeast. In a small saucepan over low heat, stir milk, water, sugar, oil, and salt until lukewarm. Add to flour mixture; beat until smooth. Blend in eggs. Beat in 1 cup flour. Stir in enough additional flour to make a moderately stiff dough. Turn onto lightly floured board. Knead until smooth, 5 to 8 minutes. Cover with pan or bowl; let rest 30 minutes.

Preheat oven to 350° F. Divide dough in half. Roll each half into a 10 x 12-inch rectangle. Spread with poppy seed filling, leaving a 1-inch margin on all sides; sprinkle with raisins. Roll up jelly roll fashion. Pinch together seam and ends. Place on greased baking sheet, seam side down. Make shallow, diagonal cuts across top. Brush top and sides of dough with egg. Sprinkle generously with poppy seed. Let rise in warm place (80°-85° F.) until doubled, about 45 minutes. Bake 30 to 40 minutes.

DESSERTS

Whole Wheat Fruitcake

Makes 1 large fruitcake

2 cups whole wheat flour
½ cup all-purpose flour
¼ cup wheat germ
1 teaspoon baking soda
2 eggs, beaten
1 can (14 ounces) sweetened
   condensed milk
1 cup pitted dates
1 cup raisins
1 cup chopped dried apricots
½ cup chopped dried pineapple
2 cups candied orange peel
1 cup filberts

Preheat oven to 300° F. Butter a 9-inch springform or tube pan. In a medium bowl, mix together whole wheat flour, all-purpose flour, wheat germ, and soda; set aside. In a mixing bowl, combine eggs and milk; blend well. Stir in fruits and nuts. Fold dry ingredients into fruit mixture. Pour into prepared pan. Bake for 2 hours or until center springs back when lightly touched and top is golden. Place pan on a rack; cool completely before turning out.

Brazil Nut Fruitcake

Makes one 3-pound cake

3 cups Brazil nuts (1 pound
   shelled)
2 packages (7¼ ounces *each*)
   pitted dates
1 cup maraschino cherries
¾ cup flour
¾ cup sugar
½ teaspoon baking powder
½ teaspoon salt
3 eggs
1 teaspoon vanilla

Preheat oven to 300° F. Butter a 9 x 5-inch loaf pan; line pan with waxed paper. In a large bowl, place Brazil nuts, dates, and cherries. Sift flour, sugar, baking powder, and salt over nuts and fruits; mix until nuts and fruits are coated. Beat eggs until foamy; stir in vanilla. Stir egg mixture into nuts and fruits; mix well. Turn into prepared pan; spread evenly. Bake for 1 hour and 45 minutes.

Chocolate Cream Icebox Cake

Makes 8 to 10 servings

3 squares unsweetened
  chocolate
½ cup sugar
  Dash salt
¼ cup hot water
1½ teaspoons unflavored gelatin
1 tablespoon cold water
4 egg yolks
1 teaspoon vanilla
½ cup walnuts
4 egg whites
½ cup cream
2 dozen lady fingers

In top of a double boiler, melt chocolate. Add sugar, salt, and hot water. Stir until sugar dissolves and mixture is blended. Stir gelatin into cold water. Add to hot chocolate mixture and stir until gelatin is dissolved. Cook over medium heat until mixture is smooth and thick. Remove pan from boiling water. Add egg yolks, 1 at a time, beating well after each addition. Return pan to boiling water; cook, stirring constantly, for two minutes. Stir in vanilla and walnuts. Transfer to a large bowl to cool. In a small bowl, beat egg whites until stiff peaks form. Gently fold into cooled chocolate mixture. Chill. Whip cream. Fold into chilled chocolate mixture.

Line the bottom and sides of a 10-inch springform pan with waxed paper. Arrange lady fingers on bottom and sides of pan. Pour in a ½-inch layer of chocolate mixture. Arrange lady fingers over the chocolate; top with another layer of chocolate. Add one more layer of lady fingers; top with remaining chocolate. Cut off lady fingers even with sides of pan; arrange pieces on the top layer of chocolate. Chill 12 to 24 hours.

Pumpkin Squares

Makes 18 servings

½ gallon vanilla ice cream,
  softened
1 cup pumpkin
1 cup sugar
1 teaspoon salt
1 teaspoon ginger
1 teaspoon cinnamon
½ teaspoon nutmeg
1 cup chopped, toasted pecans
36 gingersnaps
  Whipped cream
  Pecan halves

Chill a mixing bowl. Set out ice cream to soften. In a medium bowl, blend pumpkin, sugar, salt, ginger, cinnamon, and nutmeg. Stir in chopped nuts. Place softened ice cream in chilled bowl. Fold in pumpkin mixture. Line the bottom of a 9 x 13-inch pan with half of the gingersnaps. Top with half of the ice cream mixture. Cover with another layer of gingersnaps; add remaining ice cream mixture. Freeze until firm, about 5 hours. Cut into squares. Garnish with whipped cream and pecan halves.

Pecan Balls

Makes 4 dozen

1 cup margarine
¼ cup sugar .
2 cups sifted flour
2 cups pecans, broken into
    small pieces
    Confectioners' sugar
    Granulated sugar

Preheat oven to 300° F. Cream margarine, sugar, and flour. Add pecans; mix well. Shape dough into 1-inch balls. Bake on an ungreased cookie sheet 45 minutes. Stir together confectioners' sugar and granulated sugar. Roll baked cookies in sugar mixture while still hot.

Chocolate Nut Puffs

Makes 3 dozen

6 ounces semisweet chocolate
    chips
2 egg whites
⅛ teaspoon salt
½ cup sugar
½ teaspoon vanilla
½ teaspoon vinegar
¾ cup chopped nuts

Preheat oven to 350° F. Grease cookie sheet. In a small saucepan over low heat, melt chocolate; set aside to cool. In a small bowl, beat egg whites with salt until foamy. Gradually add sugar, beating until stiff peaks form. Beat in vanilla and vinegar. Fold in melted chocolate and nuts. Drop by teaspoonfuls onto prepared cookie sheet. Bake about 10 minutes.

Coconut Cake

Makes 10 servings

½ pound butter
2 cups sugar
6 eggs
12 ounces vanilla wafers,
    crushed
½ cup milk
7 ounces flaked coconut
1 cup finely chopped pecans
    Lemon Frosting

Preheat oven to 300° F. Butter and flour a 9-inch tube pan. Cream together butter and sugar. Add eggs, 1 at a time, beating well after each addition. Add crushed vanilla wafers alternately with milk to creamed mixture. Fold in coconut and pecans. Turn the batter into prepared pan. Bake for 1 hour and 15 minutes. Cake will be moist but firm. Cool 10 minutes in pan. Invert and cool on cake rack. When cake is cool, frost with Lemon Frosting.

Lemon Frosting

1¼ cups sifted confectioners'
    sugar
1 tablespoon melted butter
2 tablespoons lemon juice
    Milk

In a small bowl, blend sugar, butter, and lemon juice. Add milk to thin to a spreading consistency, if needed. Ice top of cake and let frosting drip down sides.

Mincemeat Pie

Pastry for a 2-crust pie
2 cups mincemeat
½ cup orange marmalade
2 tablespoons flour
1 tablespoon lemon juice
¼ teaspoon nutmeg
1 tablespoon butter *or*
  margarine
Milk
Sugar

Roll out half of the pastry on a floured surface to a circle 1 inch larger than an inverted 9-inch pie pan. Fit into pan; set aside remaining dough. In a mixing bowl, combine mincemeat, marmalade, flour, lemon juice, and nutmeg. Stir to blend. Turn into pie shell. Dot with butter; set aside. Preheat oven to 425° F. Roll out remaining dough; cut into lattice strips. Weave strips over top of pie; trim strips and press firmly to edge of bottom crust. Brush lattice with milk; sprinkle with sugar. Bake for 35 minutes or until crust is golden brown.

Cranberry Pie

Pastry for a 9-inch pie shell
1 can (8 ounces) pineapple
  chunks, drained; reserve juice
1 pound fresh cranberries
2 cups sugar
2 tablespoons unflavored
  gelatin
1 teaspoon grated orange peel
¼ teaspoon nutmeg
  Juice of 1 lemon
  Whipped cream
  Chopped nuts

Prepare pie shell. Roll out any remaining pastry; cut out with cookie cutters. Bake pie shell and pastry cutouts; set aside. Add water to reserved pineapple juice to equal 1 cup. In a large saucepan, combine cranberries, sugar, pineapple, pineapple juice, gelatin, orange peel, nutmeg, and lemon juice; bring to a boil. Boil 10 minutes, stirring occasionally. Cool to room temperature. Pour into pie shell. Chill pie until set. Top with pastry cutouts. Store in the refrigerator until serving time.

Pumpkin Cheese Pie

8 ounces cream cheese,
  softened
¾ cup sugar
2½ teaspoons pumpkin pie spice
½ teaspoon salt
3 eggs
1 can (16 ounces) pumpkin
1 teaspoon vanilla
  9-inch pie shell, unbaked

Preheat oven to 350° F. In a mixing bowl, beat cream cheese until fluffy. Gradually beat in sugar, spice, and salt. Add eggs, 1 at a time, beating well after each addition. Beat in pumpkin and vanilla. Pour into pie shell. Bake for 40 minutes or until a knife inserted near the center comes out clean. Chill before serving.

KITCHEN GIFTS

Honey Jelly

Makes 4 half-pints

2½ cups honey
¾ cup lemon juice
½ cup liquid pectin

In a medium saucepan, mix honey and lemon juice. Bring to a rolling boil. Add pectin; stir and boil 2 minutes longer. Ladle into half-pint jars to within ¼ inch of the top. Seal with 2-piece vacuum seal lids according to manufacturer's directions.

Peach Orange Marmalade

Makes 9 half-pints

12 to 15 peaches, peeled
 and cut into small pieces
1 whole orange, ground
1 cup maraschino cherries,
 ground
Sugar

In a large kettle, combine fruits. For every cup of fruit, add one cup sugar. Mix well. Simmer uncovered, stirring often, for about 1 hour. Ladle into half-pint jars to within ¼ inch of the top. Seal with 2-piece vacuum seal lids according to manufacturer's directions. Process in a boiling water bath for 5 minutes.

Fruit and Nut Popcorn Balls

Makes 26 balls

6 quarts popped corn
1 cup peanuts
1 cup raisins or other dried
 fruit
1 cup sugar
¾ cup light corn syrup
1 can (14 ounces) sweetened
 condensed milk
⅛ teaspoon salt
¼ cup butter *or* margarine
1 teaspoon vanilla

In a large buttered bowl, stir together popcorn, peanuts, and raisins; set aside. In a heavy saucepan, combine sugar, corn syrup, sweetened condensed milk, and salt; mix well. Cook over medium heat, stirring constantly, to 230° F. on a candy thermometer, about 30 minutes. Cool slightly. Stir in butter and vanilla; pour over popcorn mixture. Toss with a buttered spoon until popcorn is evenly coated. Set aside until warm. With buttered hands, shape into firm 3-inch balls. Let harden on buttered waxed paper.

Christmas Pudding Candy

Makes 5 pounds

1 heaping tablespoon butter
3 cups sugar
1 cup light cream
1 teaspoon vanilla
1 pound dates, chopped
1 pound figs, chopped
1 pound raisins
1 pound shredded coconut
2 cups nuts, chopped

In a saucepan, melt butter. Stir in sugar and cream. Heat until the mixture reaches the soft ball stage, 234°-240° F. on a candy thermometer. Beat until creamy. Stir in vanilla, fruit, coconut, and nuts until well mixed. Shape into a roll; wrap in a wet cloth. Wrap in waxed paper. Store in refrigerator for 2 weeks or longer to ripen.

Chocolate Fudge

Makes 4 pounds

4½ cups sugar
1 can (13 ounces) evaporated milk
2 tablespoons butter
Dash salt
12 ounces semisweet chocolate chips
¾ pound sweet cooking chocolate
1 pint marshmallow cream
2 tablespoons vanilla
2 cups chopped nuts

In a heavy saucepan, stir together sugar, evaporated milk, butter, and salt. Bring to a boil, stirring constantly. Boil 7 minutes, stirring occasionally. In a large bowl, mix together chocolate chips, sweet chocolate, and marshmallow cream. Pour in boiling syrup. Stir vigorously until chocolate melts. Blend in vanilla. Stir in nuts. Turn into a 9-inch square buttered pan. Cool; store in refrigerator to keep firm.

Almond Toffee

Makes 1½ pounds

1 cup butter
1 cup sugar
3 tablespoons water
½ cup chopped almonds, divided
12 ounces semisweet chocolate chips, divided

In a medium saucepan, combine butter, sugar, and water. Cook over medium heat until the mixture turns a caramel color and reaches 300° F. on a candy thermometer. Remove syrup from heat. Stir in ¼ cup nuts. Pour into a buttered 9 x 13-inch baking pan. Sprinkle ½ of the chocolate chips over the nuts; let stand a few minutes until chips melt. Smooth melted chips over the nuts; cover with waxed paper. Invert pan to remove candy. Spread with remaining chocolate chips; top with remaining nuts. Let cool until candy is hard. To serve, break into pieces.

Little Christmas Cookies

Makes about 7 dozen

1 cup butter
½ cup confectioners' sugar
1 teaspoon vanilla
⅛ teaspoon salt
1 cup cornstarch
1 cup sifted flour
Decorators' Frosting

Preheat oven to 375° F. Grease cookie sheets. In a mixing bowl, cream butter; gradually blend in sugar. Blend in remaining ingredients. Chill several hours. On a floured surface, roll out dough to ½-inch thickness. Cut out with miniature cookie cutters or cut into small squares, rounds, bars, and triangles. Place on cookie sheets. Bake 6 to 10 minutes. Small cookies will bake more quickly than larger ones. Frost with Decorators' Frosting.

Decorators' Frosting

2 egg whites
1½ cups confectioners' sugar
¼ cup light corn syrup
Food coloring

Beat egg whites until soft peaks form. Gradually add sugar, beating until sugar is dissolved and frosting stands in stiff peaks. Add corn syrup; beat 1 minute. Divide frosting into several portions. Color each with food coloring as desired. Add a few drops of water to thin, if necessary. Keep well covered until time to frost.

No-Cook Mint Patties

Makes 2 pounds

4½ cups confectioners' sugar
1 tablespoon corn syrup
⅔ cup sweetened condensed milk
¾ teaspoon peppermint extract
Green food coloring

In a mixing bowl, combine all ingredients. Dust hands and a breadboard with confectioners' sugar to prevent sticking. Shape dough into a roll about ½-inch in diameter. Cut into slices ½-inch thick. Place slices on waxed paper; press down edges with a fork. Let stand at least ½ hour before serving.

Index

BEVERAGES
Cappucino, 9
Christmas Punch, 11
Coffee Nog, 11
Cranberry Scoop, 9
Grapefruit Strawberry
  Frappé, 9
Hot Mulled Cider, 9
Orange Pineapple Shake, 11

BREADS
Bran Muffins, 44
Christmas Stollen, 49
Dark Pineapple Date Bread, 52
Elephant Ears, 53
Hungarian Christmas
  Bread, 53
Onion Rye Bread, 52
Plum Kuchen, 48
Sesame Potato Twist Loaf, 50
Wheat Germ French Toast, 47

DESSERTS
Brazil Nut Fruitcake, 54
Chocolate Cream Icebox
  Cake, 56
Chocolate Nut Puffs, 57
Coconut Cake, 57
Cranberry Pie, 59
Fruited Fluffy Yogurt, 44
Little Christmas Cookies, 63
Mincemeat Pie, 59
Pecan Balls, 57
Pumpkin Cheese Pie, 59
Pumpkin Squares, 56
Whole Wheat Fruitcake, 54

CANDY
Almond Toffee, 61
Chocolate Fudge, 61
Christmas Pudding Candy, 61
Fruit and Nut Popcorn Balls, 60
Honey Jelly, 60
No-Cook Mint Patties, 63
Peach Orange Marmalade, 60

EGGS AND CHEESE
Day-Ahead Cheese Soufflé, 47
Fancy Scrambled Eggs, 45
Hash Brown Quiche, 45
Mixed Vegetable Frittata, 47
Pineapple Cheese Ball, 4
Puffy Cheese Appetizers, 5
Sharp Gouda Spread, 4
Snappy Cheese Wedges, 8
Wheat Germ French Toast, 47

FRUITS AND NUTS
Hot Fruit Compote, 44
Fruit and Nut Nibble, 6
Fruited Fluffy Yogurt, 44
Ripe Olive Spread, 5
Spiced Peaches, 18

FISH AND SEAFOOD
Boston Baked Scallops, 32
Crab Stuffed Mushrooms, 6
Creamy Seafood Spread, 5
Crumb Topped Fish Fillets, 32
Elegant Fish Turbans, 33
Imperial Crab, 33
Simple Salmon Paté, 8

MEAT
Baked Ham with Peach or
  Cherry Glaze, 27
Baked Stuffed Rigatoni, 36
Beef and Noodle Casserole, 31
Chateaubriand with Béarnaise
  Sauce, 29
Cheddar Crust Meat Pies, 34
Crown Roast of Lamb with
  Sesame Rice, 28
Pork Roast with Herb
  Stuffing, 25
Roast Venison, 27
Spiced Orange Pot Roast, 29
Veal Marengo, 36
Veal Tarragon, 28

**PASTA, RICE, AND
STUFFING**
Baked Rice with Vermicelli, 41
Baked Stuffed Rigatoni, 36
Florentine Stuffing, 33
Herb Stuffing, 25
Louisiana Rice Dressing, 41
Sesame Rice, 28

POULTRY
Celestial Chicken, 24
Cheesy Turkey Casserole, 34
Chicken and Rice Salad, 20
Chicken and Yellow Rice, 24
Chicken Drumettes, 4
Cornish Game Hens with
  Orange Sherry Glaze, 22
Pheasant in Cream, 22
Sherried Chicken Livers and
  Mushrooms, 8
Wild Duck with Apple
  Stuffing, 24
Yam Shepherds Pie, 37

SALADS
Cherry Ring Mold, 21
Chicken and Rice Salad, 20
Christmas Cranberry Salad, 20
Colorful Garden Salad, 18
Copper Pennies Salad, 21
Cranberry Apple Salad, 18
Crisp Vegetable Medley, 17
Dilled Pea Salad, 20
Eggnog Holiday Salad, 17
Three Bean Apple Salad, 21

SAUCES AND GLAZES
Béarnaise Sauce, 29
Cheese Sauce, 37, 45
Orange Sherry Glaze, 22
Peach Glaze, 27
Shrimp Sauce, 33
Sour Cream Gravy, 27

SOUPS
Beef and Barley Soup, 12
Cheddar Cheese Soup, 15
Cheesy Cream of Potato
  Soup, 13
Garden Patch Meatball
  Soup, 16
Lentil Soup, 15
Mild Onion Soup, 15
New England Clam
  Chowder, 12
Oyster Bisque, 13
Savory Pork Soup, 16

VEGETABLES
Bavarian Wax Beans, 40
Carolina Yam Patties, 38
Crab Stuffed Mushrooms, 6
Crisp Vegetable Medley, 17
Easy Vegetable Quiche, 48
Florentine Scalloped
  Potatoes, 43
Hash Brown Quiche, 45
Lemony Green Beans and
  Carrots, 41
Mixed Vegetable Frittata, 47
Orange Glazed Beets, 43
Party Peas, 40
Party Potatoes, 43
Peanut Stuffed Squash, 40
Red Cabbage with
  Raisins, 38
Savory Blackeyed Peas, 38
Stuffed Tiny Tomatoes, 6
Vegetarian Moussaka, 37